SIGNING IS FUN

By Mickey Flodin

A PERIGEE BOOK

A Perigee Book
Published by The Berkley Publishing Group
A division of Penguin Putnam Inc.
375 Hudson Street
New York, New York 10014

Book design by Mickey Flodin

Cover design by Dale Fiorillo

Published simultaneously in Canada.

First edition: October 1995

The Penguin Putnam Inc. World Wide Web site address is
http://www.penguinputnam.com

Library of Congress Cataloging-in-Publication Data

Flodin, Mickey.
    Signing is fun / by Mickey Flodin.
        p.   cm.
    A Perigee book.
    Includes index.
    ISBN 0-399-52173-9
    1. American Sign Language—Handbooks, manuals, etc.
2. American Sign Language—Study and teaching.   I. Title.
HV2475.F56   1995
419—dc20   95-22018
                                                    CIP

Printed in the United States of America
15   14   13   12   11   10   9   8   7
This book is printed on acid-free paper.

Contents

Intro and Basics of Signing

Signing is *fun,* and this book will show you how to sign to your friends, family, or anyone. Signing is used every day by people who are deaf. Just like hearing people use speech, people who are deaf use signs to talk with their hands.

Some signs in this book are shown in profile view or at an angle. This was done to make them easier to learn. But, always face the person you are signing to.

First learn the basic hand shapes on page five. They are often used in signing and are mentioned in the instructions. They will help you form the signs correctly.

Then, learn the manual alphabet. Each letter of the alphabet is made with a hand shape. You'll find many of the signs easy to remember because they look like the English letter, such as L, M, N, O, and C. Once you know the manual alphabet, you can spell out words you don't know the signs for. Plus, the manual alphabet is often used for forming signs, such as a *C* hand shape.

Now you are ready to learn more signs. You can start with the numbers next or the signs on page 10. You'll discover *Signing Is Fun.*

Basic Hand Shapes

***And* Hand**

Flat Hand

Open Hand

Bent Hand

Curved Hand

Closed Hand

Clawed Hand

The Manual Alphabet

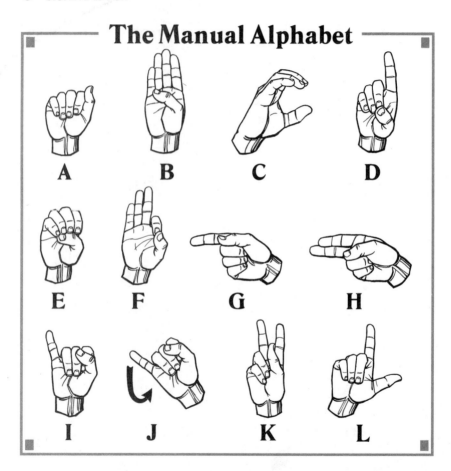

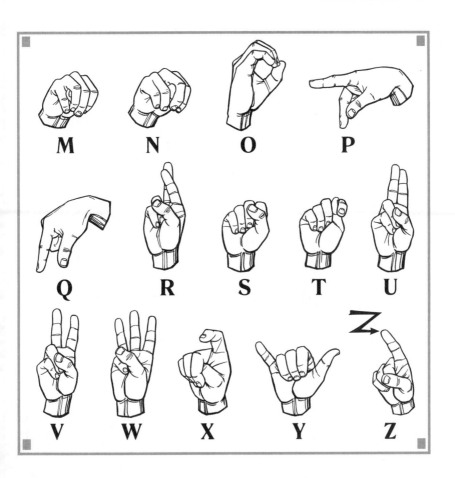

Fingerspelling Names

Fingerspelling Position
Put your hand like this to fingerspell.

D A V I D

M E G A N

K E V I N

Numbers from 0–10

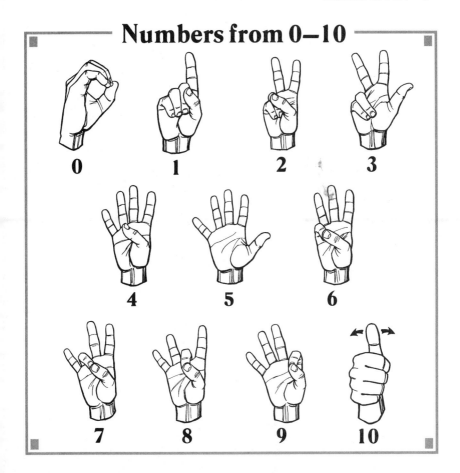

Mother

Touch the thumb of the right open hand against the chin.

Father

Touch the thumb of the right open hand on the forehead.

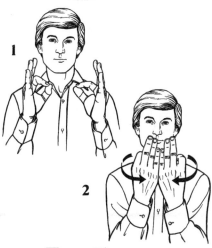

Family

Make both *F* hands face each other. Then circle both hands forward until little fingers touch.

Love

Cross the *S* hands at the wrists over the heart.

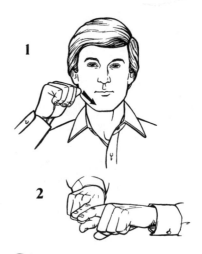

Baby

Pretend to be holding and rocking a baby.

Sister

Slide the thumb of the extended *A* hand along the right side of the jaw. Place both index fingers together.

Chair

Place the right *H* fingers on the left *H* fingers.

Bed

Put both flat hands together and place them on the right cheek.

Telephone

Hold the thumb of the right *Y* hand to the ear.

Television

Fingerspell *T* then *V*.

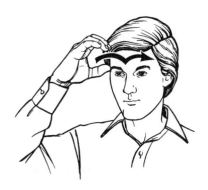

Computer

With the *C* hand, make a double arc from right to left in front of the forehead.

Radio

Place the cupped hands over the ears.

Write

Pretend to be writing on the left flat palm with the right index finger and thumb.

Read

Point the right *V* fingers at the left flat hand and move the *V* hand down.

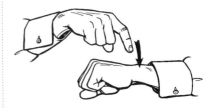

School

Clap the hands two times.

Time

Tap the left wrist a few times with the right curved index finger.

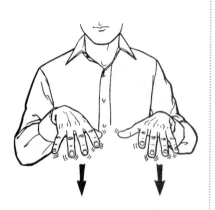

Rain

Wiggle the fingers of both hands as they move down.

Water

Touch the right side of the mouth with the index finger of the right *W* hand a few times.

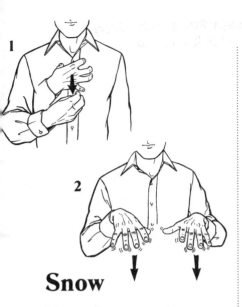

Snow

Place the curved open hand on chest. Move it forward to an *and* hand. Next move the open hands down as the fingers wiggle.

Tree

Hold the right hand upright with the left hand under the right elbow and wiggle the fingers of the right hand.

Red

Move the right index finger down over the lips.

Yellow

Move the right *Y* hand to the right while shaking it.

Blue

Move the right *B* hand to the right while shaking it.

Green

Move the right *G* hand to the right while shaking it.

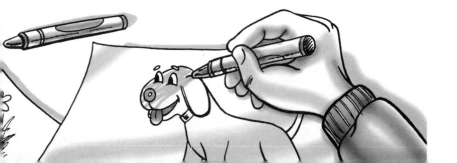

Yes

Move the right *S* hand up and down.

No

Touch the right middle and index fingers with the thumb.

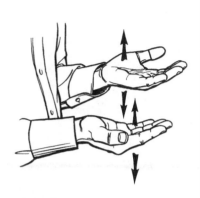

Maybe

Move the flat hands up and down alternately.

Ask

Place the flat hands together and move them toward you.

PLEASE!? CAN I GO, TOO?

When

Move the right index finger around the left upright index finger. Then touch the tip of the right index finger on the tip of the left index finger.

Who

With the right index finger, make a circle in front of the lips.

Please

Put the right hand over the heart. Move the hand in a small circle.

Thanks

Smile while touching the lips with the fingertips of both flat hands. Move the hands forward until palms are up. One hand can be used.

Hi.

Place the right *B* hand at the forehead and move it to the right. Or fingerspell *H–I*.

Good

Touch the lips with the right flat hand. Then bring the right hand down into the left hand with both palms up.

morning.

Hold the left hand flat and near the right elbow. Move the right flat hand until it is straight up.

night.

Place the right curved hand over the flat horizontal left hand.

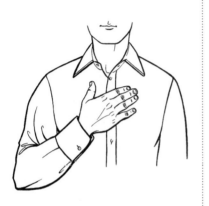

My

Place the right flat hand on the chest.

name

Cross both *H* fingers.

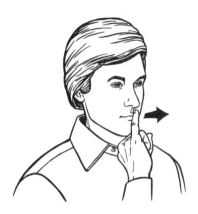

is

Move the right *I* hand forward from the mouth.

__ __ __ __ __.

Fingerspell your name.

How

Place both bent hands together back to back. Turn them forward until both hands are flat with palms up.

old

Pretend to be grabbing a beard. Then move the right hand down from under the chin ending with an *S* hand.

are

Move the *R* hand forward from the lips.

you

Point to the person you are signing to. Move the hand from left to right if there is more than one person.

?

Draw a question mark in the air with the index finger. Don't forget the dot.

Where

Shake the right index finger back and forth.

do

With both *C* hands pointing down, move them together to the left, then to the right.

you

Point to the person you are signing to. Move the hand from left to right if there is more than one person.

live?

Move the L hands up the chest together.

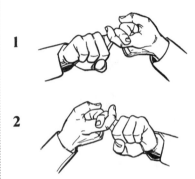

Cute

Move the *U* fingertips over the chin one or two times.

Friend

Hook the right index finger over the left index finger, then reverse the movement.

I love you.

Hold up the right hand with the thumb, index finger, and little finger extended.

Sorry

Make a circle over the heart with the *A* (or *S*) hand.

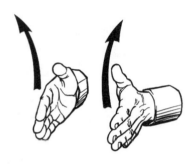

Let's

Face both open hands several inches apart. Then move them up and outward together.

play

Hold up the Y hands. Shake them back and forth at the wrists.

a

Move the *A* hand a little to the right.

game.

Bring the knuckles of both *A* hands together from the sides of the chest.

Roller Skating

Move the curved *V* hands, with palms up, back and forth alternately.

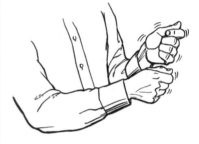

Fishing

Pretend to be holding a fishing rod and move it backward and forward.

Playing Cards

Pretend to be dealing out cards.

Tennis

Move the *A* hand back and forth as if playing tennis.

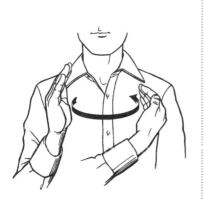

Our

Move the slightly cupped right hand in a semicircle from the right side to the left side of the chest.

team

Begin with *T* hands facing, then move them in a circle until the little fingers touch.

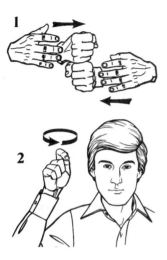

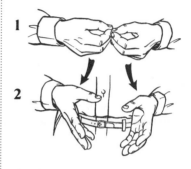

won.

Bring open hands together forming *S* hands, one over the other. Then make small circles with the raised index fingertip and thumb tip touching.

lost.

Touch the fingertips of both *and* hands. Then drop them as the hands open.

Match the Sport Signs

Each of the signs on these two pages is a sport. They are listed below. Can you guess the sports' names? Write the name in each box under the sign. The answers are on page 95. How many were you able to match?

SPORTS
Skiing
Baseball
Hockey
Basketball
Wrestling
Soccer
Football

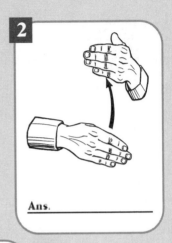

2

Ans. _____

1

Ans. _____

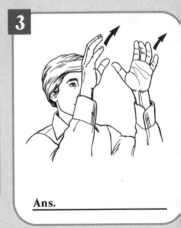

3

Ans. _____

4

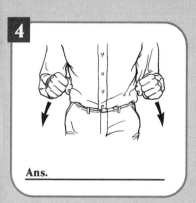

Ans. _____

5

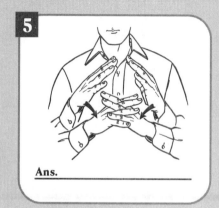

Ans. _____

6

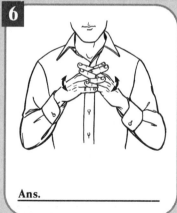

Ans. _____

7

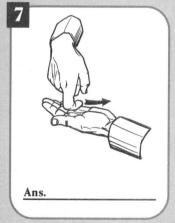

Ans. _____

Favorite

Touch the chin a few times with the right middle finger.

Camp

Touch *V* fingertips in the shape of a tent and pull them down and apart. Do this a few times as the hands move to the right.

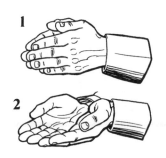

Store

Point both *and* hands down and move them in and out a few times.

Book

Close both flat hands palm to palm, then open them.

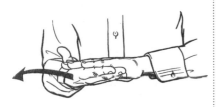

Run

Place both flat hands together palm to palm with left hand on top. Then quickly move the right hand forward.

fast.

Flip the right thumb from the bent index finger.

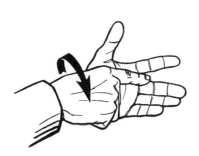

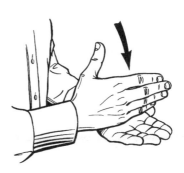

Start

Twist the right *one*
hand index finger in the
V shape of the flat left
hand.

Stop

Hit the flat left palm
with the little finger
of the right flat
hand.

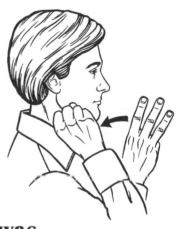

Swimming

Point the hands forward and make the motion of swimming.

was

Move the *W* hand backward and close it to an *S* hand.

fun.

Brush the nose with the
right hand *U* fingers.
Then brush the left and
right *U* fingers against
each other a few times.

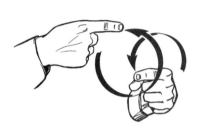

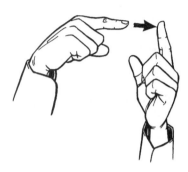

Come

Circle the index fingers as they move toward the body.

to

Hold up the left index finger and touch the left index fingertip with the right index fingertip.

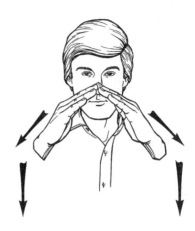

grandmother's

Touch the chin with
the thumb of the right
open hand. Move it
forward in two small
arcs.

house.

Outline the shape of a
house with the flat
hands.

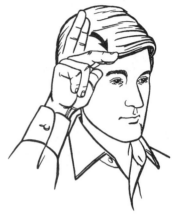

Zoo

Draw the letter Z with the right index finger on the left open palm.

Horse

Place the thumb of the right U hand on the right temple and bend the U fingers up and down a few times.

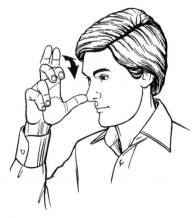

Bird

Place the right *Q* hand at the side of the mouth. Open and close the index and thumb a few times.

Bug

Touch the nose with the thumb of the right *3* hand. Then bend and unbend the index and middle fingers a few times.

Guess the Wild Animals

Each of the signs on these two pages is an animal. There is a hint under each sign. Can you guess the animals' names? The answers are on page 95.

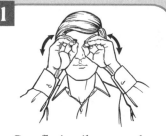

Can fly in silence and hunts at night. Who-o-o do you think it is?

Climbs and swings in the treetops.

The king of the jungle.

This reptile carries its house with it wherever it goes.

5

Is big, furry, strong, and loves honey.

6

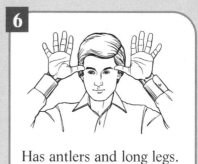

Has antlers and long legs.

7

Is smart, strong enough to lift a heavy log, and has big ears.

8

Can leap far and travel fast.

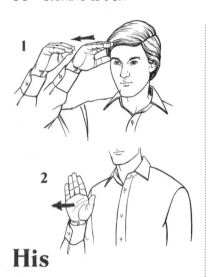

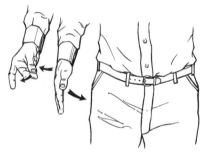

His

Pretend to be gripping a cap with the right hand. Push the flat hand, palm forward, toward the person you are referring to. If the person is there, omit gripping a cap.

dog

Slap the right hand against the right leg and snap the fingers.

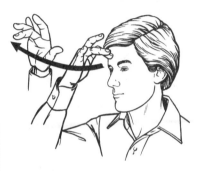

acts

Move the *A* hands in circles toward the body like pedaling a bike.

smart.

Touch the forehead with the middle finger of the right open hand. Then turn the hand forward and up.

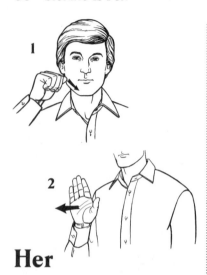

Her

cat

Trace the jaw with the thumb of the *A* hand. Next push the flat hand, palm forward, toward the person you are referring to. If the person is there, omit tracing the jaw.

Place the thumbs and index fingers of both *F* hands under the nose. Move them sideways as if touching whiskers.

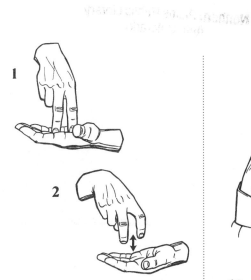

jumps.

Place the right *V* fingers in the left flat palm. Make the *V* fingers jump up and down.

climbs.

With curved *V* hands facing, make a climbing motion, one hand over the other.

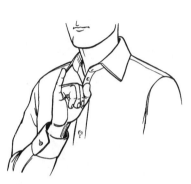

I

Place the right *I* hand on the chest with the palm facing left.

like

Place the thumb and index finger of the right open hand on the chest. The thumb and index finger are held an inch or two apart. Move the hand forward while closing the thumb and index finger.

dinosaurs.

Point the left flat hand to the right with palm facing down. Rest the right elbow on the back of the left hand with the right arm held up. Move the right bent *and* hand back and forth a few times.

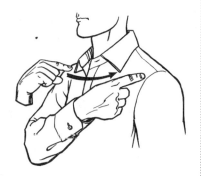

We

Touch the right shoulder with the right index finger. Then, circle it forward and back until it touches the left shoulder.

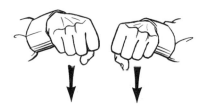

can

Move both *S* hands down together.

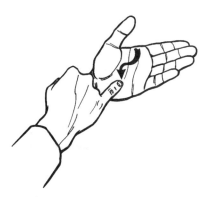

draw

Draw a wavy line on the flat left palm with the right *I* finger. The *I* finger represents a pencil.

animals.

Touch the chest with the fingertips of both bent hands. Move them back and forth sideways.

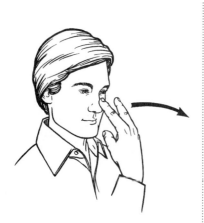

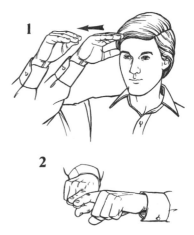

See

Point the right *V* finger-tips toward the eyes. Then move the hand forward.

brother's

Pretend to be gripping a cap. Next place the index fingers together.

new

Brush the slightly
curved right hand
across and over the
palm of the flat left
hand.

bike.

Make two *S* hands in
front of the chest with
the palms down. Then
move them in circles
like pedaling a bike.

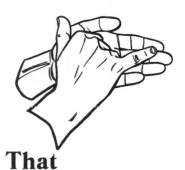

That

Place the right *Y* hand in the left palm.

dress

Place the fingertips of the open hands on the chest. Then move them down and repeat.

looks

Point the *V* hand to the eyes. Next twist the *V* hand and point it forward.

pretty.

Place the fingertips of the *and* hand on the chin. Open the hand as it circles the face from right to left. End with the *and* hand near the chin.

Grandfather

Touch the thumb of the open hand on the forehead. Move the hand forward in two small bounces.

feels

Move the right middle finger of the open hand up the chest.

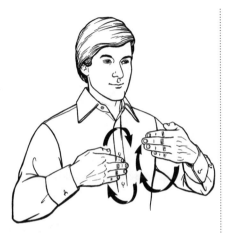

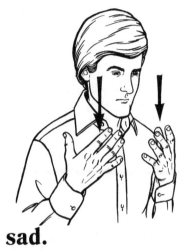

happy.

Make circles with both flat hands up and out as they touch the chest. Look happy. One hand can be used.

sad.

Place both open hands in front of the face. Drop both hands several inches while looking sad.

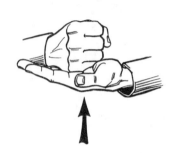

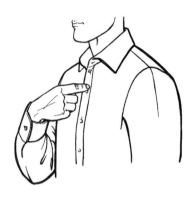

Help

Lift the right *S* hand with the left flat hand.

me.

Place the right index finger on the chest.

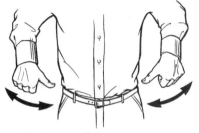

Don't

Place the thumb of the
A hand under the chin.
Move it quickly for-
ward.

show off.

Hit the sides of the
waist with both *A* hand
thumbs a few times.

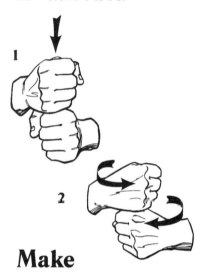

Make

Hit the left *S* hand with the right *S* hand. Twist the hands in. Then repeat.

Wish

Move the right *C* hand down the chest.

Boring

Place the tip of the index finger on the side of the nose and twist it forward.

Bad

Touch the lips with the fingertips of the right flat hand. Then turn the hand and move it down with the palm facing down.

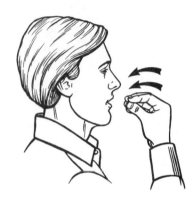

Eat

Move the fingertips of the right *and* hand to the mouth a few times.

Drink

Move the right *C* hand to the mouth as if holding a glass.

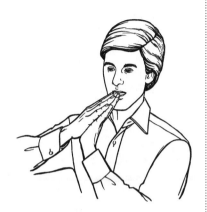

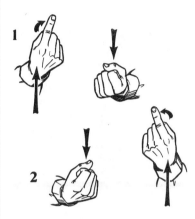

Sandwich

Put both flat hands together near the mouth.

Popcorn

Make two *S* hands with palms up. Then flip up the index fingers one after the other.

They

Point the index finger forward and move it to the right.

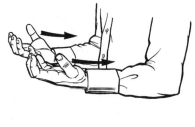

want

Hold both curved open hands with palms up. Move both hands toward the body a few times.

1

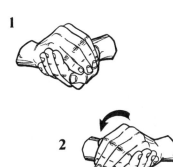

2

hamburgers.

Place the right cupped hand on the left cupped hand, then reverse.

french fries.

Sign *F* and move it to the right.

Pizza

Draw a Z shape in
the air with the right
P hand.

Spaghetti

Touch the I fingers.
Then move them apart
as they make little cir-
cles.

Chocolate

Circle the right *C* hand over the left flat hand.

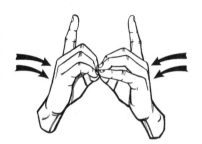

Dessert

Tap both *D* hand fingertips together a few times.

Cookie

Twist the right *C* hand fingertips in the left flat palm.

Milk

Open and close the *S* hands, one after the other, as they move up and down as if milking a cow.

Cake

Move the right *C* hand fingertips across the left flat hand.

Ice Cream

Twist the right *S* hand down near the mouth as if licking an ice cream cone.

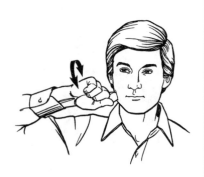

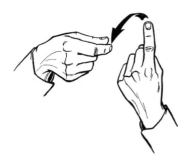

Apple

Touch the right cheek
with the right *S* hand
extended knuckle.
Twist it back and forth.

Banana

Hold up the left index
finger. Pretend to be
peeling a banana.

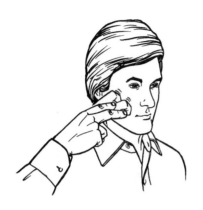

Gum (chewing)

Place the right *V* finger-tips on the cheek. Bend and straighten the *V* fingers a few times.

Candy

Move the right *U* finger-tips down the lips and chin a few times.

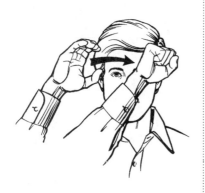

Guess

Move the *C* hand in
front of the forehead,
ending with an *S* hand.

what?

Move the tip of the
right index finger across
the left flat palm.

Vacation

Place the thumbs at the armpits and wiggle the fingers.

Money

Tap the back of the right *and* hand in the left palm a few times.

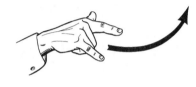

Ride (in a vehicle)

Make an *O* with the left hand. Place the right curved *U* fingers into it. Move both hands forward.

Airplane

Move the *Y* hand, with index finger extended, in the air.

Car

Make two *S* hands. Pretend to be steering a car.

Boat

Move both cupped hands forward in a wavy motion.

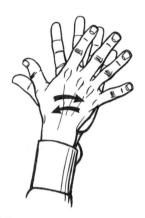

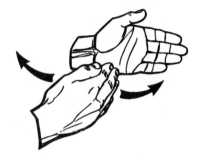

Movie

Face the palm of the left open hand almost forward. Place the right open hand on the left hand and move the right hand back and forth.

Music

Swing the right flat hand back and forth in front of the left flat hand.

Parade

Place the bent left open hand in front of the right bent open hand. Swing them from side to side as both hands move forward.

Fireworks

Hold the *S* hands with palms facing forward. Open and close each hand as they move up and down one after another.

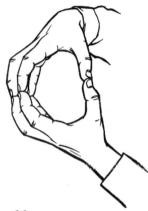

Ball

Touch the fingertips of both curved open hands in the shape of a ball.

Balloon

Hold both *C* hands in front of the mouth with palms facing. Move the hands in a circle until the little fingers touch.

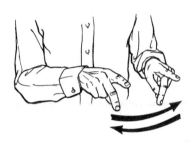

Birthday

Move both flat hands upward. The vertical right *1* hand moves down and rests on top of the horizontal left *1* hand.

Party

Swing the *P* hands left and right with palms down.

Valentine

Draw a heart shape over the heart with the *V* hands.

Day

Hold left arm flat, index finger pointing right. Place the elbow of the bent right arm on left index finger. Move the right arm, index finger up, across the body until it rests on the left arm.

GAME ANSWERS
**Match the
Sport Signs**
Pages 42–43

1. Baseball. 2. Soccer.
3. Basketball. 4. Skiing.
5. Football. 6. Wrest-
ling. 7. Hockey.

**Guess the
Wild Animals**
Pages 54–55

1. Owl. 2. Monkey.
3. Lion. 4. Turtle.
5. Bear. 6. Deer.
7. Elephant.
8. Kangaroo.